Pyotr Ilyich
TCHAIKOVSKY
SWAN LAKE
Suite from the Ballet
OP. 20A
Edited by
Carl Simpson

Study Score
Partitur

SERENISSIMA MUSIC, INC.

PREFACE

Although Tchaikovsky seriously considered extracting an orchestral suite from *Swan Lake* in 1882, there is no evidence that this idea was brought to fruition in the composer's lifetime. The ballet's premiere had been more or less successful, remaining in the Bolshoi Theatre's repertoire until 1883. Tchaikovsky's publisher issued a piano reduction of the complete ballet prepared by Nikolai Kashkin to coincide with the opening night (Feb. 20, 1877). Overall, an impressive achievement for an emerging composer in Alexander II's Russia.

Tchaikovsky was nevertheless quite aware of the fleeting success of ballet scores, and thought that an orchestral suite might help to preserve some of the outstanding music found in the complete ballet score. Thus on September 20th 1882, with the Bolshoi performances in their final season, the composer wrote his publisher, Pyotr Jurgenson, suggesting a suite from *Swan Lake*.

> "You know that the French composer *Delibes* has written ballets. Since ballet is a thing without firm foundations, he made a concert *suite* from it. The other day I thought about my own *Swan Lake*, and I wanted very much to save this music from oblivion, since it contains some fine things."
>
> [Letter 2113, English translation by Brett Langston, published on page 404 of Poznansky and Langston's *The Tchaikovsky Handbook*. Bloomington, Indiana University Press, 2002.]

Jurgenson agreed to the idea and responded shortly thereafter by sending him a copy of both the full score (in manuscript at the time) and of the piano reduction. There is no evidence of further correspondence mentioning a suite, and certainly no publication of one, for the remainder of the Tchaikovsky's life.

The revival of *Swan Lake* at St. Petersburg's Maryinsky Theatre in January 1895, with a revised libretto by the composer's brother Modest, brilliant new choreography by Marius Petipa and Lev Ivanov, and a considerably re-arranged score by the Maryinsky's resident conductor Riccardo Drigo (1846-1930), propelled the ballet into the permanent repertoire. Jurgenson issued the full score the same year in the composer's original version, though Modest's revised libretto and the three Op. 72 piano pieces orchestrated by Drigo are included.

The orchestral suite for *Swan Lake*, designated as Op. 20a, appeared for the first time in November of 1900. Jurgenson issued the suite in four different formats: Full score (Plate No. 25803, 102 pages), parts (Plate No. 25804), an arrangement for piano four-hands (Plate No. 25805B, 61 pages), and an arrangement for piano solo (Plate No. 25262, 33 pages). As first published, Op. 20a consisted of six movements:

1. Scène (No. 10 – Act II)
2. Valse (No. 2 – Act I)
3. Danse des Cygnes (No. 13, Var. IV – Act II)
4. Scène (No. 13, Var. V: "Pas d'Action" – Act II, abridged)
5. Czardas – Danse Hongroise (No. 20 – Act III)
6. Scène (No. 28, plus the first 26 bars of No. 29 Finale – Act IV)

The fact that No. 4 was cut to 100 measures (the "Pas d'Action" is 146 measures in the original ballet) with a new 7-bar codetta added, plus the merging of No. 28 and the first 26 measures of the Finale is evidence that the suite's compilation was more than a simple mechanical action of the publisher extracting sections from a large score, renumbering movements and pages, etc.

A musician of some ability would have been required to compile the suite as first published. It is presently unknown whether the musician in question was the composer himself or another, perhaps Riccardo Drigo. An examination of the score for the 1895 Petipa/Ivanov/Drigo re-working, published only in a piano arrangement by Eduard Langer, reveals a different abridgement of the "Pas d'Action" – now retitled "13. Scène" (pages 81-87): Instead of being cut to 100 measures, the movement in the Petipa/Ivanov/Drigo score omits four additional bars (38-39 and 60-61) from the original work – leaving only 96 measures. An altogether different 7-bar codetta was added. Drigo's supposed arrangement of the 1900 suite is therefore open to question.

To make matters even more complicated, Muzgiz (the Soviet State Music Publisher) issued a different, eight-movement suite from *Swan Lake* in 1954. This score was clearly reproduced from the original Jurgenson plates, though a fair number of typographical modifications were made. (The complete ballet was re-engraved in 1957 for the Tchaikovsky *Collected Works*.) This score stands at 125 pages of music in contrast to the original suite's 102. The compiler of this second version is anonymous, and the rationale for its compilation unknown. This score was the one reprinted and issued by Kalmus as No. A2185 prior to the present edition. While the first five movements are identical with those of the original suite, the final movement was omitted and three dances from the ballet were added:

6. Danse Espagnole (No. 21 – Act III)
7. Danse Napolitaine (No. 22 – Act III)
8. Mazurka (No. 23 – Act III)

The present edition is based upon the composer's autograph of the ballet score (in microfilm), an early published edition of the ballet full score (Jurgenson, Plate No. 4432), the first edition of the suite (Jurgenson, Plate No. 25803), and the Kalmus reprint of the 1954 Soviet version of the suite. The two-volume 1957 Soviet *Collected Works* full score of the ballet was also consulted. The editor of the present edition has elected to restore the final movement of the original suite to its rightful place at the end while retaining the three wonderful dance movements that were added to the Soviet score. Movement titles from the original ballet score have been restored, with the last movement (No. 9) now designated as "Scène et Finale." While the duration for all nine movements in the present suite adds up to approximately 35 minutes, it is easily possible to perform either of the two previous versions of the suite from the present edition via the simple omission of selected movements.

January, 2006   *Carl Simpson*

CONTENTS

1. Scène 5
2. Valse 13
3. Danse des Cygnes 42
4. Pas d'Action 46
5. Czardas – Danse Hongroise 55
6. Danse Espagnole 67
7. Danse Napolitaine 82
8. Mazurka 93
9. Scène et Finale 110

Movements 1 through 5 are present in both the 1900 and 1954 versions of the Suite. Movements 6 through 8 were added for the 1954 version, while the last movement, which is present in the 1900 version, was omitted.

ORCHESTRA

Piccolo, 2 Flutes, 2 Oboes, 2 Clarinets, 2 Bassoons

4 Horns, 2 Cornets, 2 Trumpets, 3 Trombones, Tuba

Timpani, Triangle, Bass Drum, Cymbals, Tambourine, Castanets

Harp

Violin I, Violin II, Viola, Violoncello, Bass

Duration: ca. 35 minutes

SWAN LAKE
Suite from the Ballet
Op. 20a
1. Scène

Pyotr Ilich Tchaikovsky (1840-1893)
Edited by Carl Simpson

* Original keys: Trumpets in F, Cornets in A

© Copyright 2006 Carl Simpson.
All rights reserved.

* Violin I, mm. 26/4-27/1-3: Figure is written an octave higher in the autograph.

*Violins, Viola, mm. 39, 41: Doubling Flutes, Horns in the autograph.

10

*Strs.(except Bass), mm. 56-59: No tremolando, plain half-notes only in Autograph.

12

2. Valse

14

*Cello, Bass, m. 35: The "pizz." indication starts at m. 36 in the autograph.

17

18

*Cl. 2, mm. 97-98: No indication of which player in autograph. From analogous spot in mm. 94-95.

21

22

24

27

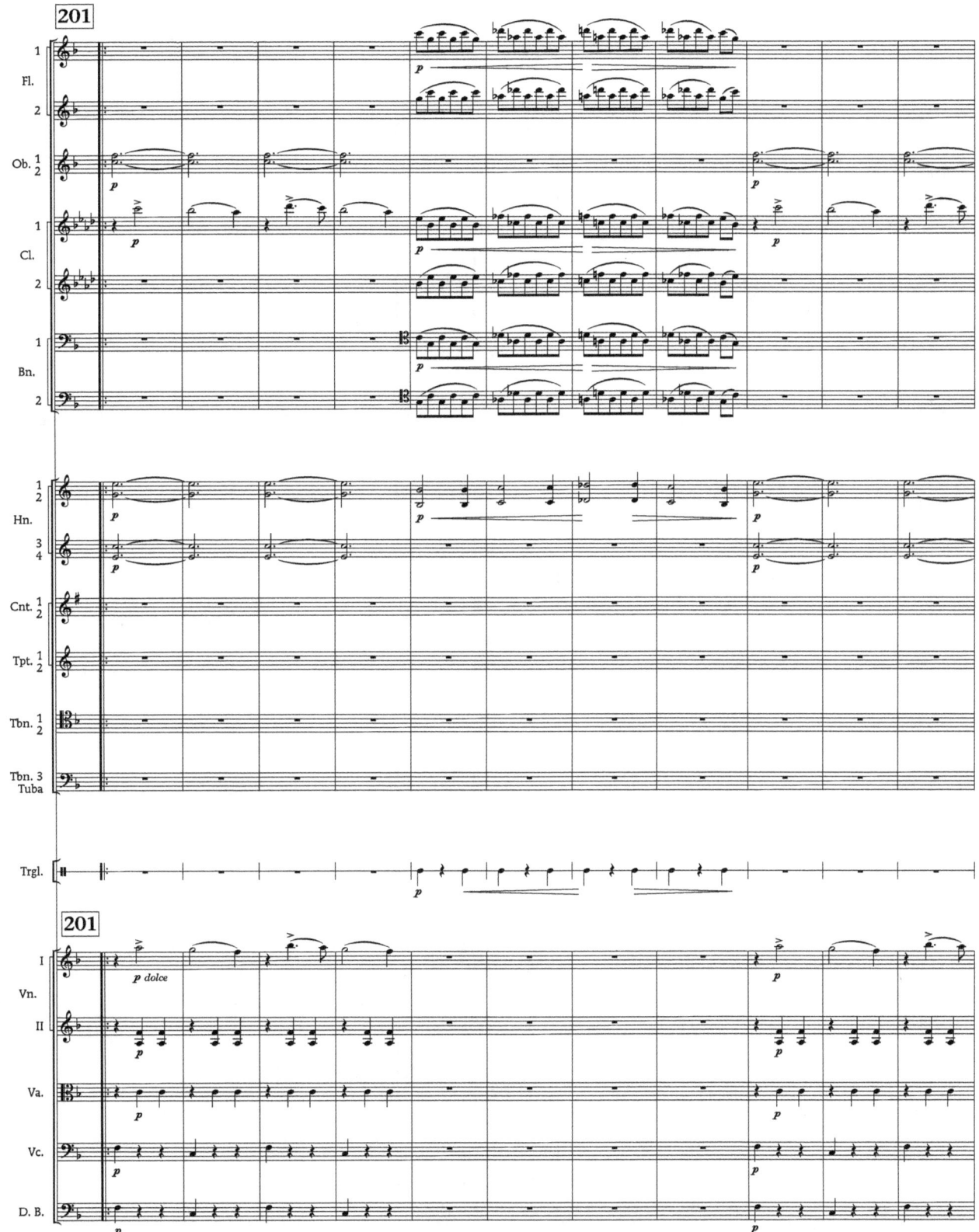

*Violin I, Viola, m.225: Autograph has B♭ - F double stop in Violin I, with only the lower F in Viola.

30

*Timpani, mm. 351-352: D in the autograph instead of A.

40

*Bn, 2, m. 391/2: Autograph has lower octave.

3. Danse des Cygnes

4. Pas d'Action
(Odette et le Prince)

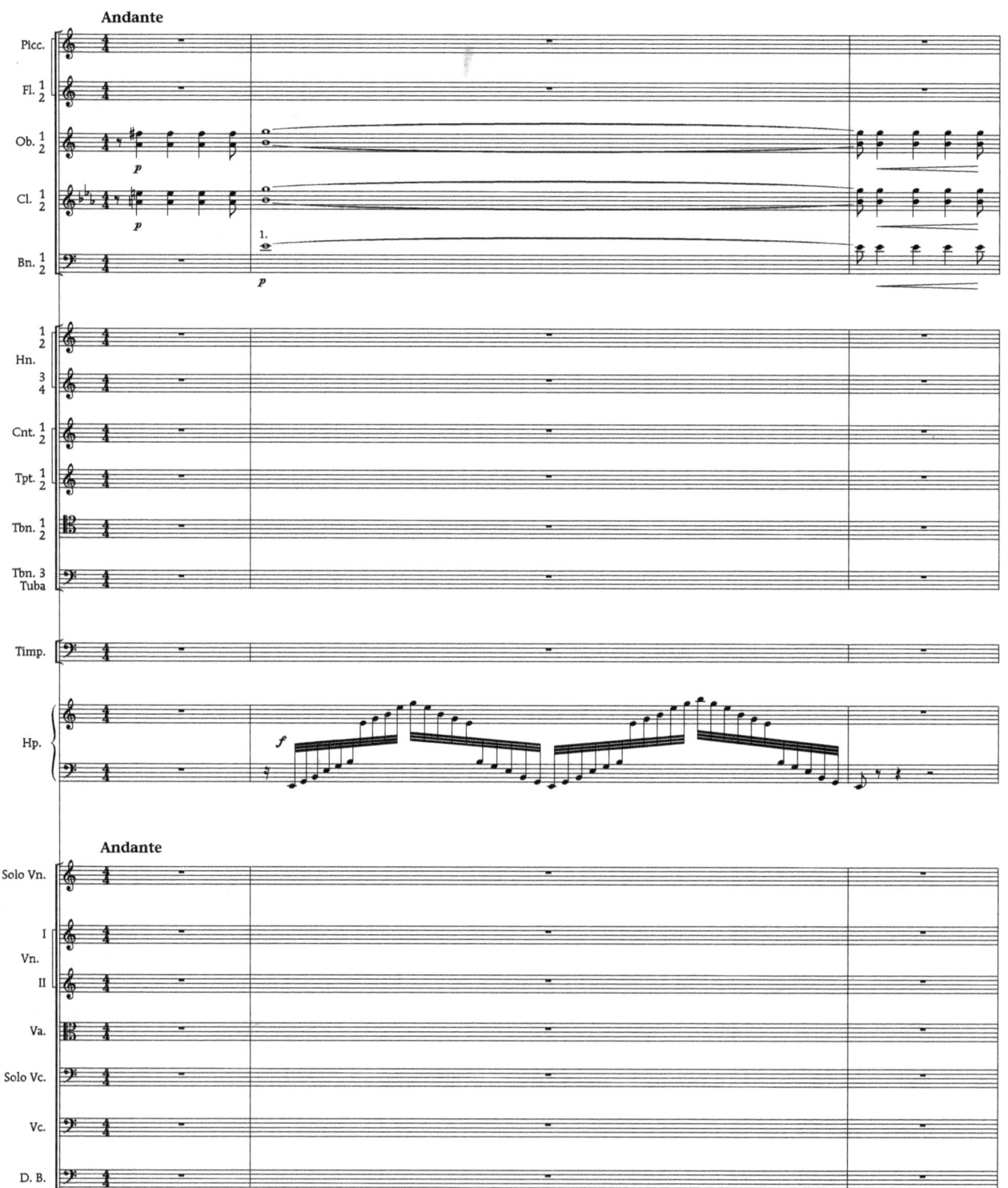

48

*Solo Violin, m. 12-13: The slur starts on the last note of bar 12 in the autograph.

**Harp, mm. 24-34: Arpeggio indications are absent in the autograph.

49

50

* The final 46 measures of this movement from the original ballet score have been cut. The present ending (mm. 101-107), altogether absent from the ballet score, was possibly added by the anonymous compiler of the Suite shortly prior to its publication in 1900 by Jurgenson.

5. Czardas – Danse Hongroise

* *Violins, Cello, Bass, mm. 17-20: The final eighth-note of the triplet figure in beat two is tied to the following quarter-note (unaccented) in the first editions of both the ballet and orchestral suite.*

* Bassoons, mm. 30, 32: The tie connecting the half-note in Bn. 1 is absent in the autograph. Likewise, the slur ends on the second beat in Bn. 2. The present edition follows Jurgenson here.

* (See note on previous page)

64

*6. Danse Espagnole

* This dance was not included in the first edition of the orchestral suite.

** Flutes, Clarinets, m. 4 and all later parallels: In the autograph, dots are present only in measure three. They were included in first editions of the ballet and orchestral suite.

* Viola, mm. 15,16: The final eighth-note is an A in the autograph.

* Clarinets, m. 24 (also m. 33): The lower notes of the 2-note figures are F and D in the autograph.

72

* (See note on page 66)

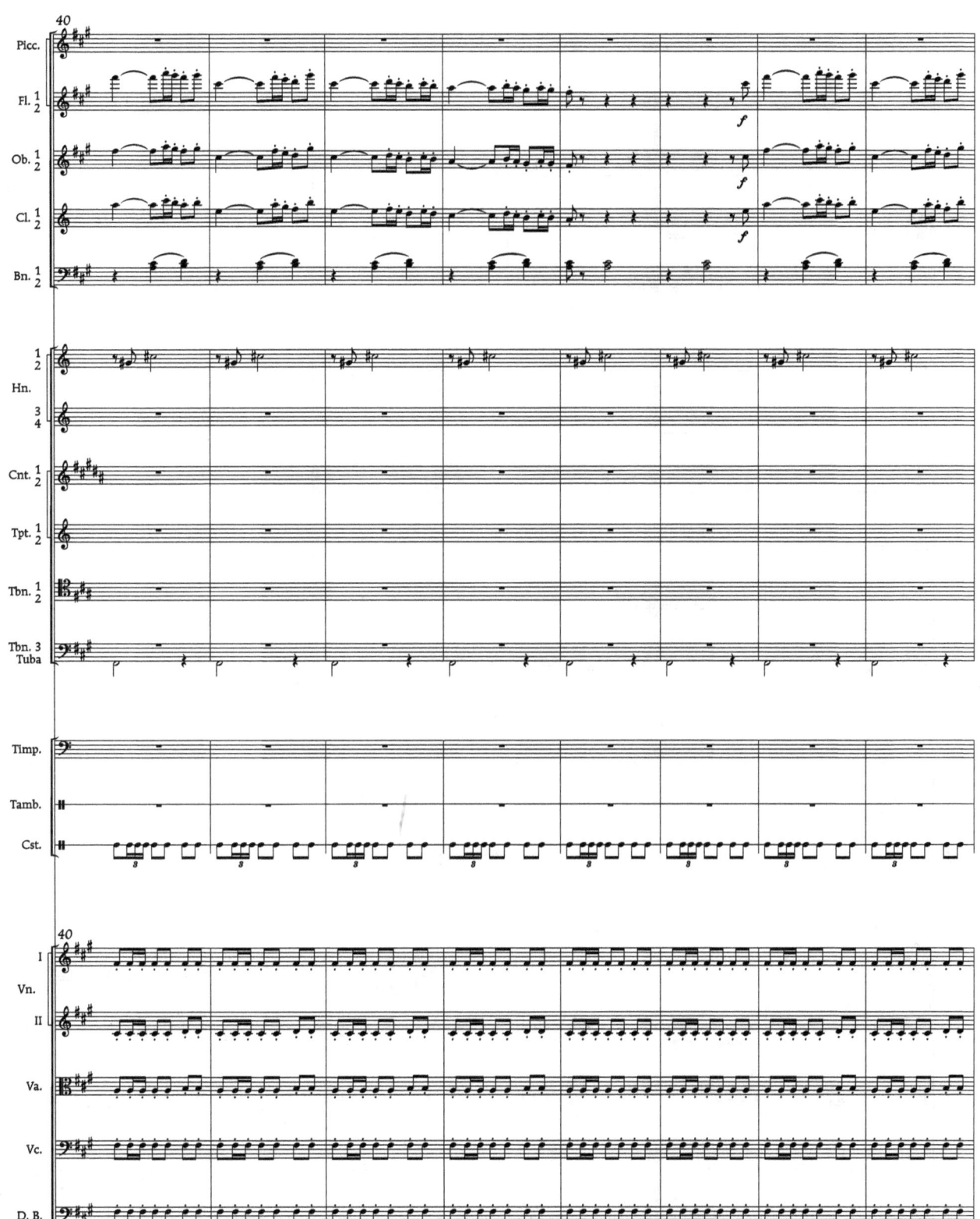

*Woodwind (except Bns.), m. 50: This measure was left blank in the autograph.
The first edition has been followed here.

* Cornets, mm. 82–83: These measures were left blank in the autograph.
The first edition has been followed here.

* Viola, m. 91 (also 95): This measure was left blank in the autograph. The first edition has been followed here.

80

* (See note on previous page)

**Trumpets, m. 96 (also 98): The first notes are F♯, G♯ in the autograph.
The first edition full score has been followed here.

* Measures 98-99 are absent in the autograph. However, they appear in both the first editions of the piano reduction (arr. Nikolai Kashkin, 1877) and full score.

*7. Danse Napolitaine

* This dance was not included in the first edition of the orchestral suite.
** Timpani, m. 1: The first ed. of the full score adds a roll to both notes.

*** Bassoons, mm. 3-4: These measures are blank in the autograph.
**** Cornet, mm. 6-23 (and later parallels): The dots are taken from the first edition full score. They are absent in the autograph.

* Violin I, m. 10: In the autograph, beat two is given the two eighth-notes (small notes).

84

* Cornet, m. 23/1: This is written as a eighth-note in the first edition.

86

91

92

* Woodwind (except Bns.), Cornets, Violins, mm. 88-90: The slurs are absent in the autograph and have been supplied from the first edition of the full score.

*8. Mazurka

* This dance was not included in the first edition of the orchestral suite.

** Oboes, mm. 7-8 (also 41-42, 120-121, 152-153):
In the autograph, these two measures originally doubled the Flutes.

*Violin II, m. 10 (also mm. 43, 123, 131, 155): The lower A is written as a quarter-note in the autograph.

**The slurs are missing in the autograph

*Ob. 2, m. 31: Autograph has D (small notes)

99

* *Cymbals, m. 77: This measure is absent in the autograph and has been supplied from the first edition full score.*

103

* Woodwind (less Bsn.), Horns 1-2, Viola, m. 170/1: The composer originally wrote a dominant (D-major) chord here. Flute 2, Oboes, Clarinets and Violas had the notes of beat 2 on the first beat as well, while the Horns 1-2 had E-C♯. Tchaikovsky corrected the Viola staff in his autograph. The remaining corrections appear in the first edition.

* Cymbal, Bass Drum, m. 172: The small notes are present in the autograph and omitted from the first edition.

* Cornet 2, m. 192: The autograph has a written F
(concert D) here. The C♯ (B) is from the first edition.

9. Scène et Finale

112

* Hn. 1, m. 31: This measure is blank in the autograph. The note is taken from the first edition.
** Bass, m. 32: The small notes are present in the autograph, but crossed out.

117

122

*Viola, m. 84: The first edition gives only the lower note (B♯) of the double-stop.

125

128

* Harp, m. 109: The autograph repeats measure 108 here.

www.ingramcontent.com/pod-product-compliance
Lightning Source LLC
Chambersburg PA
CBHW080516110426
42742CB00017B/3139